AF599208

Community Workers

Doctors

by Amy McDonald

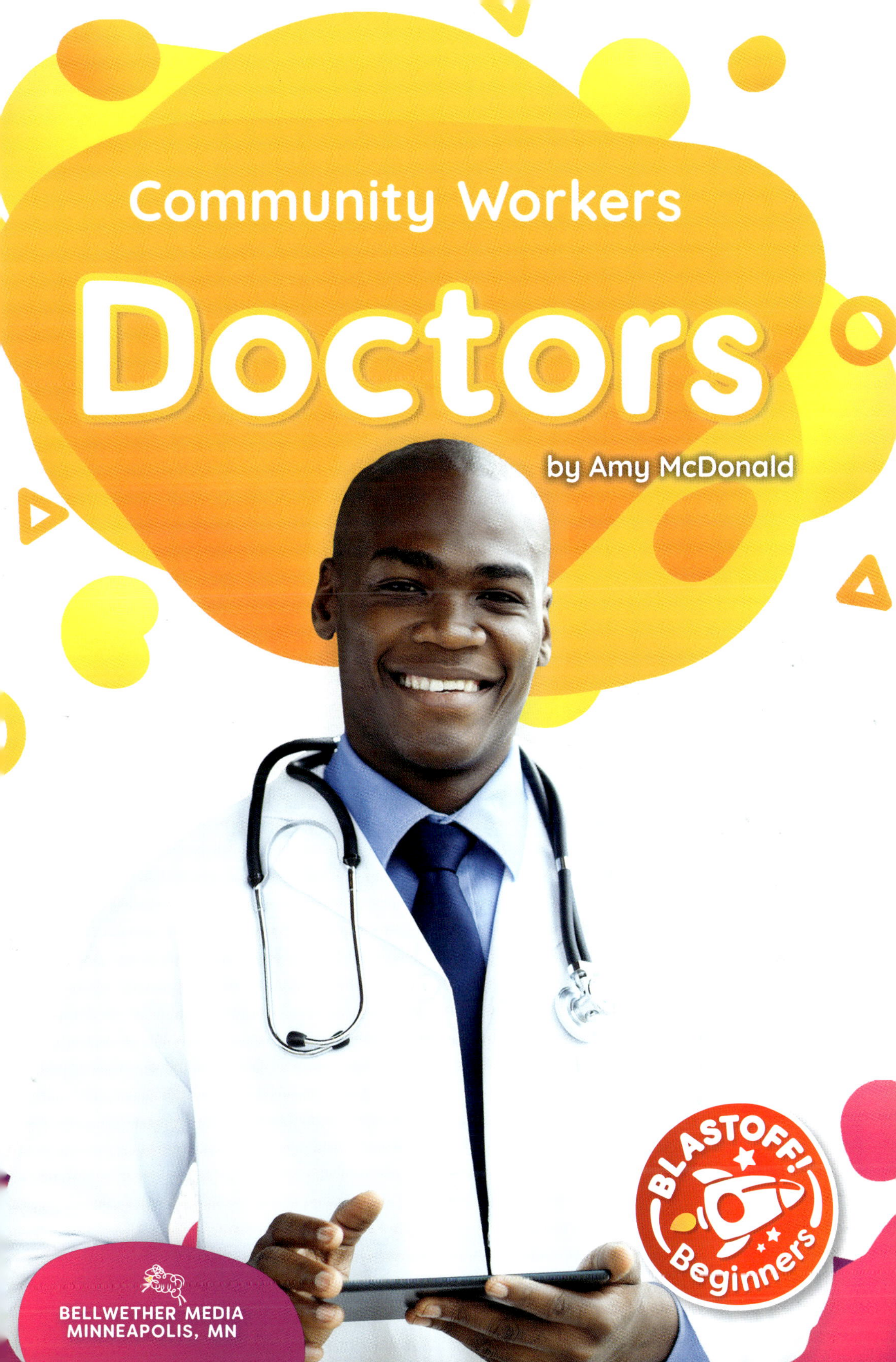

BELLWETHER MEDIA
MINNEAPOLIS, MN

Blastoff! Beginners are developed by literacy experts and educators to meet the needs of early readers. These engaging informational texts support young children as they begin reading about their world. Through simple language and high frequency words paired with crisp, colorful photos, Blastoff! Beginners launch young readers into the universe of independent reading.

Sight Words in This Book

and	is	they
are	look	use
do	people	white
help	some	who
in	the	will

This edition first published in 2025 by Bellwether Media, Inc.

Library of Congress Cataloging-in-Publication Data

LC record for Doctors available at: https://lccn.loc.gov/2024004947

Editor: Betsy Rathburn Designer: Laura Sowers

Printed in the United States of America, North Mankato, MN.

Table of Contents

On the Job

Ana is sick.
The doctor
will help!

What Are They?

Doctors help people who are hurt or sick.

They work in **clinics**. They work in **hospitals**.

clinic

hospital

They wear
white coats.
Some wear
masks and gloves.

What Do They Do?

Doctors do checkups. They look in eyes and ears.

They stop sickness.
They give **shots**.

shot

They clean cuts.
They use
bandages.

bandage

They help fix
broken bones.

Why Do We Need Them?

Doctors work hard. They help us feel better!

Doctor Facts

Tools

A Day in the Life

look in eyes
and ears

give
shots

clean
cuts

Glossary

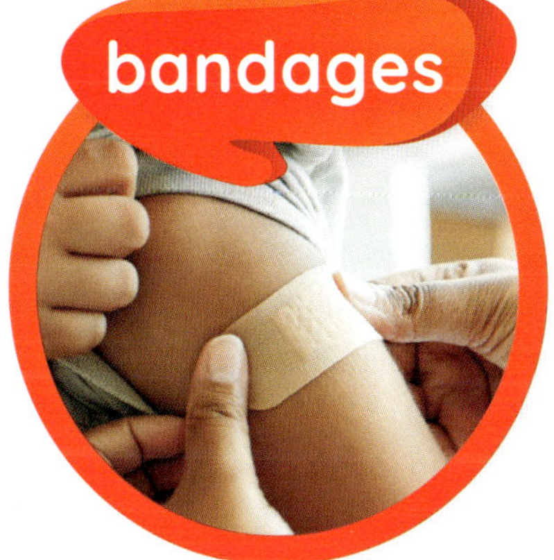

bandages

coverings used on cuts

clinics

places where people get checkups

hospitals

places where doctors help sick or hurt people

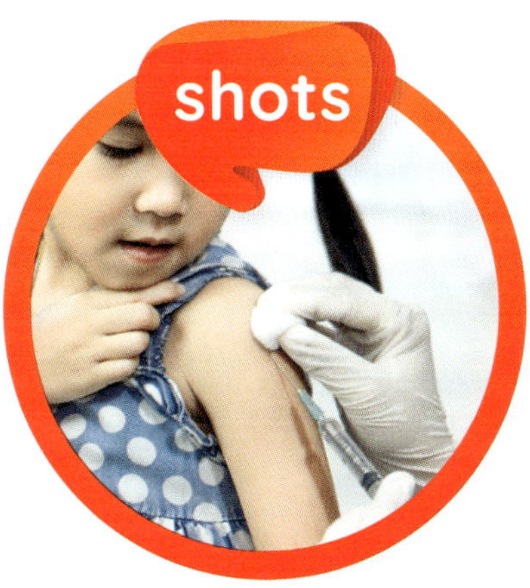

shots

medicines given with needles

To Learn More

ON THE WEB

FACTSURFER

Factsurfer.com gives you a safe, fun way to find more information.

1. Go to www.factsurfer.com.
2. Enter "doctors" into the search box and click 🔍.
3. Select your book cover to see a list of related content.

Index

The images in this book are reproduced through the courtesy of: michaeljung, front cover, pp. 6-7; New Africa, pp. 3, 22 (masks, give shots); wavebreakmedia, pp. 4-5; FatCamera, p. 8 (clinic); Gorodenkoff, pp. 8-9, 23 (hospitals); YoloStock, p. 10 (mask, glove); Sakdawut Tangtongsap, pp. 10-11; paulaphoto, pp. 12-13; Jacob Lund, pp. 14-15; SofikoS, pp. 16-17; SDI Productions, pp. 18-19; AnnaStills, pp. 20-21; Supa Chan, p. 22 (gloves); Pixel-Shot, p. 22 (bandages); Serhii Bobyk, p. 22 (look in eyes and ears); Elnur, p. 22 (clean cuts); PeopleImages - Yuri A, p. 23 (bandages); Peakstock, p. 23 (clinics); A3pfamily, p. 23 (shots).